HAUNTED PRISONS

A Crabtree Branches Book

THOMAS KINGSLEY TROUPE

Crabtree Publishing
crabtreebooks.com

School-to-Home Support for Caregivers and Teachers

This high-interest book is designed to motivate striving students with engaging topics while building fluency, vocabulary, and an interest in reading. Here are a few questions and activities to help the reader build upon his or her comprehension skills.

Before Reading:

- *What do I think this book is about?*
- *What do I know about this topic?*
- *What do I want to learn about this topic?*
- *Why am I reading this book?*

During Reading:

- *I wonder why...*
- *I'm curious to know...*
- *How is this like something I already know?*
- *What have I learned so far?*

After Reading:

- *What was the author trying to teach me?*
- *What are some details?*
- *How did the photographs and captions help me understand more?*
- *Read the book again and look for the vocabulary words.*
- *What questions do I still have?*

Extension Activities:

- *What was your favorite part of the book? Write a paragraph on it.*
- *Draw a picture of your favorite thing you learned from the book.*

TABLE OF CONTENTS

Dead Cells 4
Ohio State Reformatory 6
Moundsville State Penitentiary 8
Lawang Sewu, Indonesia 12
Eastern State Penitentiary 14
Tihar Jail, India 18
Old Beechworth Gaol, Australia 20
Bodmin Jail, United Kingdom 22
Alcatraz, San Francisco 24
Conclusion 28
Glossary..30
Index 31
Websites to Visit 31
About the Author......................................32

Dead Cells

You walk down the long corridor, barely able to see the way ahead. The cells on either side of you are empty and abandoned. Somewhere in the distance, you hear footsteps scrape. A shadow moves between the nearby bars. An icy feeling comes over you as you realize you're not alone. Is this old prison as haunted as they say?

Many believe ghosts can haunt any sort of location imaginable. Prisons and jails are where criminals are sent as punishment. Maybe some prisoners are sentenced for life...and the afterlife.

Grab your flashlight and take a deep breath. You're about to discover why these prisons are among... THE HAUNTED.

FRIGHTENING FACT

There are more than 10 million people in prison around the world.

OHIO STATE REFORMATORY

The front of Ohio State Reformatory in Mansfield, Ohio, doesn't look like a prison. It looks like a fancy castle. Built in 1896, it closed in 1990.

In the basement of the prison, a 14-year-old boy died. His shadow often appears on the walls. Another more **sinister** ghost appearing there is the guard who killed him.

Ohio State Reformatory has been used as a location in a number of Hollywood movies. The most popular film is *The Shawshank Redemption*, based on a short story written by popular horror author Stephen King.

MOUNDSVILLE STATE PENITENTIARY

Known as one of the most violent prisons in the United States, Moundsville State **Penitentiary** was built during the civil war. Murders, **riots**, and hangings took place within the property.

After decades of overcrowding and **inhumane** living conditions, the prison closed in 1995. Paranormal investigators have heard voices in the dark, silent cell blocks. Footsteps can be heard where no one was walking.

It's no wonder Moundsville is haunted. There were close to a thousand prisoners who died or were executed over the prison's dark history. To make matters even creepier, the facility was rumored to have been built on an ancient Native American burial ground. The graves were likely disturbed once construction began.

In 1951, electrocution became the preferred method of execution at Moundsville. Of the 94 men **executed**, 9 of them were electrocuted in the electric chair nicknamed "Old Sparky." West Virginia outlawed executions entirely in 1965. Old Sparky sits on display at the prison.

LAWANG SEWU, INDONESIA

Lawang Sewu was built originally as a headquarters for the Dutch East Indies Railway in 1907. During World War II, the Japanese invaded Indonesia and turned Lawang Sewu into a prison. There, many prisoners were executed.

Visitors to the historic spot have seen headless ghosts wandering the corridors. Photos taken there sometimes reveal unexplained figures in the background.

FRIGHTENING FACT

A woman who died at the site is believed to haunt the building too. Some believe her ghostly image was captured on an Indonesian TV show recorded at Lawang Sewu.

Eastern State Penitentiary

Along busy Fremont Avenue in Philadelphia stands a crumbling building that seems out of place. It looks like a dark and foreboding castle with towers and high walls. The building is Eastern State Penitentiary, which opened in 1829.

The prison used cruel methods to make their prisoners behave. Inmates were left alone in small, cramped cells with little light.

A number of famous criminals served time in Eastern State Penitentiary, including notorious **Mafia** boss Al Capone. He was caught outside a movie theater carrying an unlicensed gun. His stay at Eastern State was his first time in jail. Because of his power and **influence**, his cell wasn't like any of the others. It had fancy furniture, rugs, paintings, and a radio.

Over time, Eastern State's methods for correcting prisoner behavior was stopped. The facility had too many prisoners and was closed in 1971.

The prison is considered one of the most haunted places in America. Visitors to the historic location have heard voices and laughing. Shadowy figures and ghostly faces appear on the walls. Many have noticed the shape of a guard in one of the towers.

FRIGHTENING FACT

Eastern State was designed to hold 300 prisoners. By the 1920s they were forced to lock up around 2,000 inmates!

TIHAR JAIL, INDIA

Tihar Jail in India is their largest complex of prisons. It is spread over 400 acres (162 hectares) and holds around 16,000 prisoners. Unlike the other prisons mentioned in this book, Tihar Jail is still open!

Some inmates there claim the prison is haunted. They've heard ghostly wails in the middle of the night. Others have been mysteriously slapped, and some prisoners saw the ghosts of past criminals who were hanged.

OLD BEECHWORTH GAOL, AUSTRALIA

The Old Beechworth **Gaol** is located in Beechworth, Victoria, Australia. Built in 1864, the prison was open for 140 years and was the home of a number of **notorious** criminals and murderers.

One of the most famous prisoners was Ned Kelly, who was an outlaw and gang leader. He served time at Beechworth for the murder of three police officers.

Ned Kelly

Beechworth closed as a prison in 2004. A year later, the location opened back up as a historical site and for ghost tours.

Visitors have reported hearing voices in the dark when no one in the group was talking. Others have seen mysterious figures that seem to watch them from afar. Lights have been known to turn off and on by themselves, too.

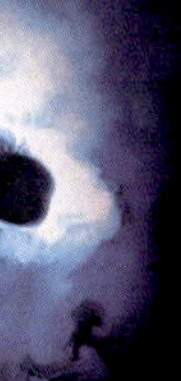

FRIGHTENING FACT

In the late 1800s, eight men were sentenced to death for murder. They were hanged outside of the prison.

BODMIN JAIL, UNITED KINGDOM

Bodmin Jail was built in 1778, in Cornwall, Great Britain. It was the first jail where prisoners had their own cells.

Some claim Selina Wadge, who was hanged for throwing her baby down a well, haunts the prison. Young visitors to the jail have seen a ghostly woman in a long dress crying in a jail cell.

Mannequins are used to portray a prisoner receiving his last rites before his execution.

FRIGHTENING FACT

Bodmin Jail held outdoor public hangings until 1862. The hangings were very popular and many people came to watch them. After 1862, the hangings were held inside.

ALCATRAZ, SAN FRANCISCO

One of the most famous prisons in the world is on an island of its own...seriously! Off the coast of San Francisco, California, is Alcatraz Island, home to Alcatraz Federal Penitentiary.

The prison opened in 1934 and was built near an old military prison that still stands today. Alcatraz was considered the place to send prisoners who were too dangerous for other jails.

Unlike many other haunted prisons, Alcatraz was only open for a little under 30 years. It closed in 1963 and later became a **tourist** attraction.

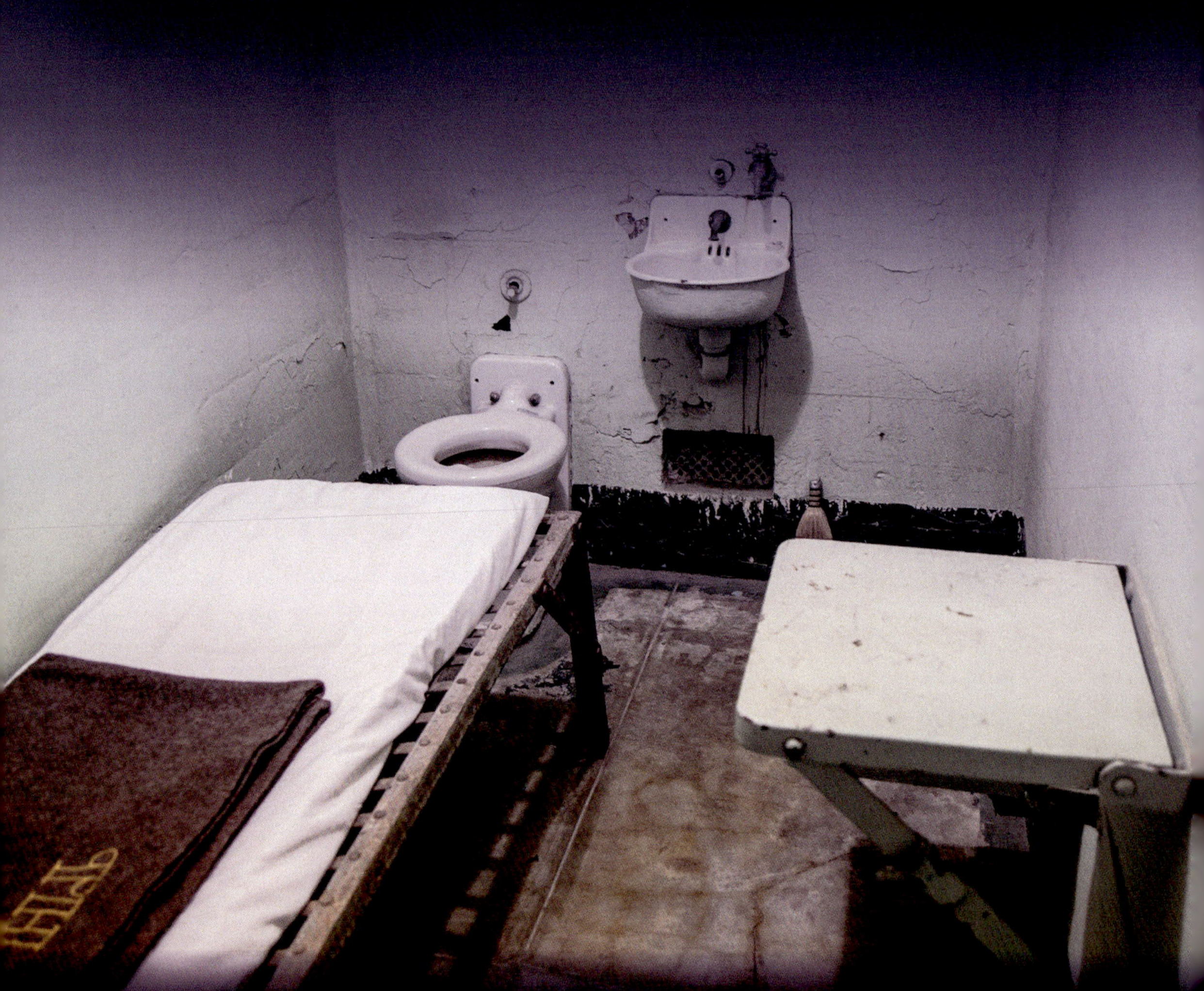

People claim to hear ghostly crying and moaning in cell blocks A, B, and C. Others have sworn they heard banjo music playing in the empty showers. Ghostly Native Americans killed during the Civil War sometimes appear and whisper to the living.

The most haunted spot in Alcatraz is believed to be the D-Block. Cell 14-D is otherwise known as "the hole"—a place where difficult prisoners were kept as punishment. The cell is always cold, even during the heat of summer. Visitors to "the hole" have mentioned feeling a sudden intense presence from the area.

CONCLUSION

Are the ghosts imprisoned in these jails stuck there for eternity? What one person sees, another might explain away.

It's up to you to decide for yourself. If you hear or see something creepy, write it down or capture it with a camera. The evidence you discover might bring us closer to understanding...THE HAUNTED.

GLOSSARY

executed (EK-suh-kyoot-ed): To be put to death according to a legal order

gaol (JAYL): British spelling for the word "jail"

influence (IN-floo-uhnss): Power to affect another person

inhumane (in-hyoo-MAYN): Cruel treatment

Mafia (MAH-fee-uh): An organized crime group that makes money from illegal activity

notorious (noh-TOR-ee-uhss): Well known for bad characteristics

penitentiary (pen-uh-TEN-chur-ee): A public institution, jail, or prison that confines prisoners

riots (RYE-uhtz): Public violence and disorder

sinister (SIN-uh-stur): Twisted and evil behavior

tourist (TOOR-ist): Someone who visits other locations for pleasure or culture

INDEX

Alcatraz 24, 25, 26, 27
Capone, Al 15
Eastern State (Penitentiary) 14, 15, 16, 17
ghost(s) 5, 7, 13, 19, 21, 23, 28
graves 10
inmates 15, 17, 19
Kelly, Ned 20
murders 8, 20, 21
Tihar Jail 18–19
Wadge, Selina 23
World War II 12

WEBSITES TO VISIT

https://kids.kiddle.co/Ghost

www.hauntedrooms.co.uk/ghost-stories-kids-scary-childrens

www.ghostsandgravestones.com/how-to-ghost-hunt

ABOUT THE AUTHOR

Thomas Kingsley Troupe

Thomas Kingsley Troupe is the author of a whole pile of books for kids. He's written about ghosts, Bigfoot, werewolves, and even a book about dirt. When he's not writing or reading, he investigates the paranormal as part of the Twin Cities Paranormal Society. He lives in Woodbury, Minnesota with his 2 sons.

Crabtree Publishing

crabtreebooks.com 800-387-7650

Produced by: Blue Door Education for Crabtree Publishing
Written by: Thomas Kingsley Troupe
Designed by: Jennifer Dydyk
Edited by: Kelli Hicks
Proofreader: Crystal Sikkens
Production manager: Candice Campbell
Prepress technician: Katherine Kantor

Hardcover	978-1-4271-5558-0
Paperback	978-1-4271-5564-1
Ebook (pdf)	978-1-4271-5570-2
Epub	978-1-4271-5576-4
Read-along	978-1-4271-5582-5
Audio book	978-1-4271-5588-7

Printed in the U.S.A./072025/CP20250722

Published in Canada
Crabtree Publishing
616 Welland Avenue
St. Catharines, Ontario
L2M 5V6

Published in the United States
Crabtree Publishing
347 Fifth Avenue
Suite 1402-145
New York, NY 10016

The images/photos depicting "ghosts" in this book are artists' interpretations. The publisher does not claim these are actual images/photos taken of the ghosts mentioned in this book.

Photographs: Cover photos: prison cells © Freaktography, prisoner © FOTOKITA, skull on cover and throughout book ©Fer Gregory, pages 4-5 creepy picture borders here and throughout book © Dmitry Natashin, page 4 © Chingfoto, page 5 hands shadow © sakhorn, page 6 © Sandra Foyt, page 7 © Shanelb, pages 8-9 © Steve Heap, page 10 © Raeann Davies, page 12 © Andreas H, page 14 © Inspired By Maps, page 15 (top) © MISHELLA, (bottom) © agel Photography, page 16 © MISHELLA, page 17 © Chang Lee, page 18 © mrinalpal, page 19 © kittirat roekburi, page 21 © Nils Versemann, page 22 © Editorial credit: Paolo Trovo / Shutterstock.com, page 23 (top) © Paolo Trovo, (bottom) © RogerMechan, page 24 © f11photo, page 26 © Lerner Vadim, page 28 © Tunatura, page 29 © Paul W. Faust, All images from Shutterstock.com except page 9 and 11 photos released into the public domain by its author, VitaleBaby at the Wikipedia project, page 13 basement photo © Crisco 1492 https://creativecommons.org/licenses/by-sa/3.0/deed.en, page 20 © public domain image, page 25 © Steffen https://creativecommons.org/licenses/by/3.0/deed.en, page 27 © bennymarty/istockphoto.com

Library and Archives Canada Cataloguing in Publication

Title: Haunted prisons / Thomas Kingsley Troupe.
Names: Troupe, Thomas Kingsley, author.
Description: Series statement: The haunted! | "A Crabtree branches book". | Includes index.
Identifiers: Canadiana (print) 20210220228 | Canadiana (ebook) 20210220236 | ISBN 9781427155580 (hardcover) | ISBN 9781427155641 (softcover) | ISBN 9781427155702 (HTML) | ISBN 9781427155764 (EPUB) | ISBN 9781427155825 (read-along ebook)
Subjects: LCSH: Haunted prisons—Juvenile literature. | LCSH: Ghosts—Juvenile literature.
Classification: LCC BF1477.3 .T76 2022 | DDC j133.1/22—dc23

Library of Congress Cataloging-in-Publication Data

Names: Troupe, Thomas Kingsley, author.
Title: Haunted prisons / Thomas Kingsley Troupe.
Description: New York, NY : Crabtree Publishing Company, [2022] | Series: The haunted! - a Crabtree Branches book | Includes index.
Identifiers: LCCN 2021022536 (print) | LCCN 2021022537 (ebook) | ISBN 9781427155580 (hardcover) | ISBN 9781427155641 (paperback) | ISBN 9781427155702 (ebook) | ISBN 9781427155764 (epub) | ISBN 9781427155825
Subjects: LCSH: Haunted prisons--Juvenile literature. | Ghosts--Juvenile literature.
Classification: LCC BF1477.3 .T76 2022 (print) | LCC BF1477.3 (ebook) DDC 133.1/22--dc23
LC record available at https://lccn.loc.gov/2021022536
LC ebook record available at https://lccn.loc.gov/2021022537